EXPLORING CAREERS IN
TV AND FILM

Directing in
TV and Film

Cavendish
Square

New York

Published in 2019 by Cavendish Square Publishing, LLC
243 5th Avenue, Suite 136, New York, NY 10016

Library of Congress Cataloging-in-Publication Data

Names: Graham, PJ.
Title: Directing in TV and film / PJ Graham.
Description: New York : Cavendish Square, 2019. | Series: Exploring careers in TV and film | Includes glossary and index.
Identifiers: ISBN 9781502640536 (pbk.) | ISBN 9781502640543 (library bound) | ISBN 9781502640550 (ebook)
Subjects: LCSH: Television--Production and direction--Juvenile literature. | Motion pictures--Production and direction--Juvenile literature. | Television--Production and direction--Vocational guidance--Juvenile literature. | Motion pictures--Production and direction--Vocational guidance--Juvenile literature.
Classification: LCC PN1992.75 G73 2019 | DDC 791.4502'32--dc23

Editorial Director: David McNamara
Editor: Kristen Susienka
Copy Editor: Rebecca Rohan
Associate Art Director: Alan Sliwinski
Designer: Christina Shults
Production Coordinator: Karol Szymczuk
Photo Research: J8 Media

Printed in the United States of America

CONTENTS

Directors are magic makers and miracle workers. Do you have what it takes to be one?

CHAPTER ONE

Do You Have What It Takes?

L ights, camera, action!" Do you want to be the person saying these words? Do you dream of bringing stories to life on the big screen? You are not alone, but a lot of work and a diverse skill set are what make becoming a director in the TV or film industry a reality and not a dream.

Overcoming the Odds

TV and film directors often say they have the best job in the world, and they could be right. They are part of a busy and imaginative industry where travel, creative collaborators, and energy abound. They create a product that entertains thousands or even millions of people. What could be better?

However, there is another side to a directing career. It is incredibly competitive and demanding. It requires a lot of decision making and leading. The work of becoming a director doesn't end when a filmmaker finally lands his first feature film. Even with one movie under a director's belt, many never direct a second film.

According to studies, 54 percent of white male directors never make a second movie, and 80 percent of white female directors are in that same category. For directors of color, male or female, the percentage goes up another 3 percent to 8 percent. While there is clearly some gender and racial imbalance in the industry, it also shows that a lot of people either aren't hired to make a second film or don't want to make another.

So, how does someone beat these odds? Doing two things helps:

1. Understanding what a director truly does, which is a lot more than directing the camera shots during a show or movie production.

2. Learning and developing the skills and traits needed to succeed—starting now.

Anyone who dreams of being a great director needs this toolbox and the right attitude, especially if they want to attract great actors, cinematographers, film editors, and other professionals to work with.

Directing Chaos Into a Funnel

There is no typical day for a director. The ability to work flexibly is part of the job. As a director, you might shoot in the middle of the night in freezing temperatures or on a scorching hot afternoon. You could be on location in New Zealand or Georgia or on a set in Hollywood or Vancouver. You could help an actor with a question about his or her character one minute and handle an emergency with the stunt coordinator the next minute.

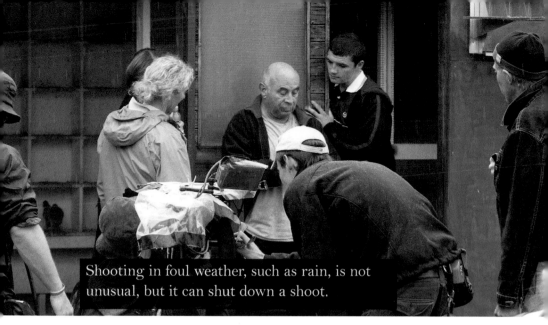

Shooting in foul weather, such as rain, is not unusual, but it can shut down a shoot.

Filmmakers must handle stress and a lot of decision making. Matthew Arnold, cofounder of RocketJump Film School and director of the comedy web series *Video Game High School,* says that directing is like "directing chaos into as tight of a funnel as you can."

Shooting a television show or film requires a ton of organization and focus. While most of us watch and see a logical progression of the story, directors cannot shoot in that logical order. They have to divide a scene into shots, which is any time the camera angle or the light angle moves. If a scene were shot in order as it happens, lighting and camera crew would be doing a ton of extra work moving lights and cameras back and forth. Instead, the director and his or her assistants plan in advance to get as many shots as possible done before moving a camera and lights to a new angle.

Every time both the camera and lights have to be moved, it's called a turnaround. Reducing turnarounds helps keep a production on schedule and on budget.

Every time a scene is shot, the director must make the call to either reshoot it or decide if the shots they

Setting up cameras and lights takes time, so a director works to reduce turnarounds.

have capture what is needed for the story. The director has to balance his or her creative vision with the funding and the time available.

Considering all of this, let's look at some things that a future director really needs to have a long career that they will look back on with satisfaction.

Be Confident

Confidence comes up time and time again when directors talk about what kind of people are good directors. As the director, you are the leader of the team, the coach that tells everyone how to do their job better while keeping them inspired to do so. If the director doesn't believe in himself or herself—or the story he or she is trying to tell—he or she can't expect to motivate others to give their best work. Being confident is the first step toward making cast and crew believe in the production.

Be Diligent

The path to the director's chair is often littered with obstacles and challenges. If you believe in yourself and the story you want to tell, you have to be diligent in moving past obstacles and delays on your way. Consider that the average age of a working director is in their forties. Many break out when much younger, such as Robert Rodriguez, Lena Dunham, and Peter Jackson, but most have to work their way up through the ranks.

One must also have diligence (and patience) to handle all the questions and expectations that are put upon the director's shoulders. While it's a creatively rewarding job, it has its stressful moments too. Learning to work through delays and keep working on a project in spite of problems will serve you well later!

Be on Time

Yes, being on time to the set or to meetings is important. It says that you respect others who are working on the production. Keeping the shoot on track is another way that time is important for a director. Knowing what you want before you shoot is part of it. Another part is taking the time to be prepared, planning your shots for quick turnarounds, and sticking to the schedule lined up in the call sheet. A call sheet is the document that tracks all the details about when actors arrive, when lighting is needed on set, and when cast and crew need to be on set.

This could mean that when a scene isn't going as hoped, a director may have to cut his or her losses and move on just to stay on schedule. Why is this so important? First, the time each cast member is picked up, sent to makeup, and arrives on set is carefully scheduled. The same goes for the technical crew that sets up the lights, cameras, etc. Taking too long for one scene could affect shoots for days or even weeks. Second, if a lot of scenes take longer to shoot than expected, this means extra hours the crew has to be paid for, more services to feed and drive everyone, more electricity for the lights, and so on. Every delay can stress the budget. Even the leader on set has to watch how much money is being spent, or film companies may not hire him or her again.

Be an Everybody's Director

You may have heard of the term "actor's director," which means a director that has a very good understanding of how actors work and what they need to provide a great performance—and works hard to provide these things to actors. This is a good thing, but there's no reason why that kind of relationship should only be between actors and directors when it benefits most on-set relationships.

Having an idea and a style in mind doesn't mean much if the director cannot explain the idea to his or her team. Learning the terminology of the actor, cinematographer, special effects artists, and so forth is the best way for a director to ensure that they describe what they want in a way that is understood by others. Plus, learning about the other areas of the filmmaking process helps a director understand what's possible. He or she will also earn more respect from cast and crew if he or she knows what the work of each department is like.

In the video series *Film Courage*, director Jack Perez says the best way to learn how others do their work is to do it yourself when beginning. For example, he recommends that even if you plan to have a film editing student cut the film, you should cut it yourself first. Experiencing similar tasks as your coworkers helps you become a better director.

Be a Decision Maker and a Master Multitasker

Being the director means that, normally, you have the most creative control (television is a little different). It also means you have the most decisions to make. What color scheme makes sense for the wardrobe of a particular character? What kind of car should they drive? Is a filming location suitable? Is the planned stunt fall high enough? The person helming a film or show will be bombarded with questions every day. Being able to answer quickly and in line with the vision that's been established is a must. Doing this goes back to having a clear idea of what you want and doing preplanning. The questions a director faces daily also hint at the variety of tasks a director faces.

Be a Nonlinear Thinker

You've already heard that directors need to be multitaskers. They rarely get the luxury of focusing on just one thing for an extended period of time. Further, they must track a story in their head even when the shooting is taking place out of story order. This is done to save on time setting up cameras and lights as a scene with multiple angles is shot, but it requires the director to stop thinking strictly in a linear way.

Plus, they may also have to do some sequences inside a studio while others are outdoors on location—and some of those will be in order in the editing process.

Staying calm and knowing what you need for your story from day to day is key to keeping your cool as a director.

Be a Delegator, Not a Control Freak

There are some directors who take on other roles, be it screenwriter, producer, or editor, but that's not always ideal. While director James Cameron is known to write screenplays, jump behind the camera, and edit his films, not everyone should follow his lead. Often, directors learn how to do these other jobs as they learn about the industry, and it helps them communicate and understand other professionals. While you may be a good film editor as well as a good director, does that mean you will be the best editor for all your films? Probably not.

As such, it helps to learn to trust other people who are good at what they do and learn how to share your creative vision with them so they can help you make it a reality. Directors have a large team to lean on. They try to work well with others so the best people want to work with them.

Be a Passionate Storyteller

If you want to be a director, you need to be driven by one thing: the desire to tell stories! Otherwise, why do you want to do the job? Films and television shows and programs are all about telling a story that takes viewers out of the real world while simultaneously illuminating aspects of the real world. This is achieved through many different formats and genres. Whether you like comedy, drama, or horror, it all boils down to storytelling.

Telling a great story takes practice, but to become a director, you must also be passionate about sharing that story. Many directors talk about the film they did that they loved, even if it wasn't a critical or financial success. They still say it was worth making because they loved the story and believed the world needed to see it.

Getting Ready

It sounds like a tall order to become a director with a solid career, doesn't it? How do you even begin to develop all or some of the things on this list? First, don't try to do it all at once. Those who go on to become great directors usually spend years working up the ranks before they get to call "Action!" for the first time.

However, you can start learning these things in school by staying open to activities and classes that combine teamwork, multitasking, and creativity. This will be discussed in detail in chapter 3, but acting in plays or musicals, being part of a publication staff, writing original stories or screenplays, and making YouTube videos can help you build a director's "toolbox."

Above all, keep an open mind about what is available to you and go out of your comfort zone.

Directors and cinematographers are creative partners, as seen here with director Woody Allen (*left*) and cinematographer Vittorio Storaro (*right*).

CHAPTER TWO

Teamwork

The role of director sounds like a creative and powerful position, and it is. However, there is much more to the role than working with actors and calling shots from the director's chair, and there are more types of directing roles than many realize.

A Glimpse at the Job

A director is the creative leader and decision maker on a film production team, but he or she is not alone. He or she partners with the director of photography to achieve his creative vision. There are first and second assistant directors and sometimes third assistant directors, and they all require the same strong organizational and communication abilities.

Being the director for both television and film requires a lot of work, starting weeks or months before filming and going on long after filming stops. They must research and plan to make sure that all the shooting goes smoothly. They need to inspire the actors and work to make the whole cast and crew a strong team. On top of that, a director should try to be an information sponge, learning as much as possible about the technologies and techniques of the people working with them.

Hitting the Books for Research and Planning

An important piece of the puzzle in preparing a movie is research. The director must discover all he or she can about the character he or she is filming to make it realistic to the audience. Say that a movie's main character is a hotshot doctor. Every detail about the doctor, from what kind of car she drives to what her bedside manner is like, is important for properly characterizing her.

Aside from character development, subjects explored in the production may need to be better understood by the director. He may have to research filming locations to see if they meet the needs of the project and if they are affordable. He might even do research to prepare for casting.

Storyboarding

Before anything is filmed, the director and his or her assistants will storyboard the scenes. What is storyboarding? It is creating a graphic representation of how the scene will unfold, shot by shot.

Done in sequential order, the assistant director draws each shot in a small square or rectangle. It doesn't have to be well drawn; it just has to be good enough to give everyone the idea of what kind of shot it is and where the characters will be in the frame.

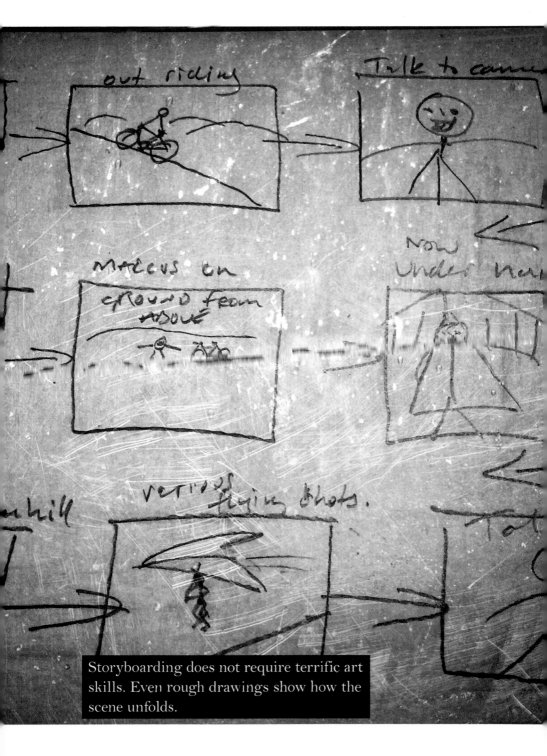

Storyboarding does not require terrific art skills. Even rough drawings show how the scene unfolds.

This might seem like a lot of work instead of just telling someone what you want, but consider the old phrase, "A picture is worth a thousand words." This is certainly true when trying to explain what your idea for a shot is. A visual example will communicate your idea much better, especially to visually oriented people like cinematographers.

Storyboarding also forces the production team to make a concrete plan for getting all the shots that they need. The process requires a shot-by-shot analysis that can be translated into a shot list.

Planning for Great Performances

Sometimes directors have to juggle a streamlined approach with tactics to get the most out of the actors' performances. It's common for directors to schedule shooting scenes that will require a lot of focus or energy earlier in the day when the cast is fresh and move less-intense scenes to the end of the day.

It also pays to have a knack for knowing how to push an actor the right way for the role. Once, director Sidney Lumet was directing actor Al Pacino in a film where Pacino's character had to make two intense phone calls. Lumet wanted to shoot both calls in one stretch because he believed that Pacino's energy and emotions would build. The problem? The scene would be fifteen minutes long, and the film cameras used at the time could only shoot eleven minutes of footage before having to be reloaded. It took several minutes to rewind and reload a camera.

Getting creative with his cameras, Lumet set up two cameras as close together as possible. They placed a black tent around the cameras so they wouldn't distract the star. The director started the shoot with one and began the second camera when the first camera was getting close to the end of the roll. He later decided to have extra film rolls and did the scene twice without stopping. The result: the emotionally exhausted performance from Pacino that Lumet had been looking for.

Picking Sets Versus Locations

Choosing where the film or TV show takes place is a big part of what can make a film look realistic—and decides whether it stays on budget.

A set is basically the film and TV version of a stage, the area created to represent the setting for all or part of the story. Set designers work hard to make these look realistic and dynamic, and they work well for the interiors of homes, businesses, and cafés. The advantage of a set is that the environment is controlled: the lighting, the temperature, the sound quality, and who is roaming around it. Another plus of a set is that you can shoot there for as long as you need to. The lights will always be on when you need them.

The downside is that sets are expensive to create, and they can look phony if they aren't done well. After all, not all directors will be handed a budget to create something like Harry Potter's Diagon Alley or the Hobbit village set from *The Lord of the Rings*, which was spread over 14 acres (5.7 hectares).

Locations are real places that are leased for use by film crews. Sometimes permits are required by the town in order to film there. This is usually a less expensive option, and it looks real.

The disadvantage? There's little ability to control the light. After all, a director can't make the sun come out. The sound quality may be compromised if the director has to struggle to get rid of traffic sounds or other noises from the area. It can be hard to keep people who aren't in the cast or on the crew away from the location, or to secure equipment on a multiple-day shoot. Also, a location may never be exactly what the director wants, though he or she might get close.

Directors need to be ready to work in either environment, depending on the needs and budget of the project. They also have to make decisions about which to use for each part of the film to make the setting as realistic as possible without busting the budget.

Juggling these and many other tasks is much easier when a director has two things figured out: knowing what they want and knowing how the cast and crew work. It can't be said strongly enough: knowing what you want for your film will decide whether you are a good director or just a mediocre one (or a downright annoying one). How you interpret the screenplay and plan to bring it to life needs to be clear in your head before you can expect anyone else to understand how to help you. Even the most expert cinematographers and assistant directors can't help if you don't get the concept clear in your own mind.

A director must know how to do a little bit of a lot of things, to use the correct terminology of the production's departments, and to know what they can

Director Peter Jackson appears on a set of old New York City built for the movie *King Kong*.

and cannot do. While every director is new at some point, if he or she doesn't take the time to comprehend the work going on around him or her, the person won't be very effective in the director role.

It's important for the director to have a general understanding of how other people on set do their work. This helps when the director is asking for something specific, such as a certain type of filming

TRAVEL FOR WORK AND CREATIVITY

An often-cited perk of being a director—or anyone on a film set for that matter—is traveling and experiencing different countries and cultures as part of the job.

While New York City and Hollywood used to be the centers of filming, other cities and countries have stolen the limelight in recent years. Georgia, Louisiana, and even Canada's Vancouver and Toronto are hot spots for filming in North America, and there are plenty of exciting and distant locations that filmmakers have also discovered. Countries like the United Kingdom, Ireland, and New Zealand are now well known for providing some atmospheric sites for successful productions such as *Guardians of the Galaxy*, *Star Wars: The Last Jedi*, *Downton Abbey*, *Game of Thrones*, and other films and TV shows.

Less conspicuous choices also make the list. The Czech Republic has been used for more than forty US movies in recent years, including *The Illusionist* and *Casino Royale*. The television series *The Alienist* was shot in Budapest, Hungary, as were *Blade Runner 2049* and *The Martian*. France, Spain, Germany, and China are often used by Hollywood too.

People enjoy experiencing different places, but it can also boost creativity. New sights, smells, and languages can light up different parts of the brain, sparking creativity. Studies also show that international travel increases cognitive flexibility, which is the

The cast and crew of the *Lord of the Rings* trilogy worked on location in New Zealand.

mind's ability to move from one idea to another, which is linked to creativity. The key for this is to become engaged in the local culture rather than sticking to tourist destinations. So these experiences boost a director's creativity—a professional bonus of travel!

shot or a special effect. The director knows how to ask for what they want, or if it's even possible to do. Understanding acting methods and language is very helpful for any director, but so is learning how cameras operate, how digital effects can and cannot be used, and how a film is edited.

Who's Who

There is more than one type of director in film and television. On most sets, the job falls to several people, with one person being the primary director. That is the person whose vision is guiding the film from preplanning to postproduction. The assistant directors and other people support this person to achieve his or her vision. No matter what level a director is, they are all masters of multitasking and need to understand the work of—and communicate with—other film professionals, from scriptwriters and actors to special-effects artists and film editors.

First Assistant Director

Also known as the AD, the first assistant director is the director's right-hand person. The AD's role is vital, as they take care of the practical elements of shooting so the director can focus more on creative aspects and plotline. They work with the director to storyboard the shots and determine the shoot order, supervise cast and crew, ensure that the filming schedule stays on track, and remove and reduce hazards on set.

Like the director, the AD must be a leader and know how to communicate and solve problems while juggling a dozen or more tasks. On top of that, he or she needs to have strong organizational skills. During preproduction, the AD will handle storyboarding, create the filming schedule, and ensure that locations, props, and equipment are hired or rented.

On a production day, he or she ensures that everyone is ready when the director needs them and that the shooting is on schedule. The first assistant director is also in charge of the call sheet and supervising the second and third assistant directors.

Second Assistant Director

Before cast and crew step on set, they have different processes to help them embody their characters. The second assistant director in in charge of moving cast members through makeup, hair, and wardrobe as efficiently as possible, so cast members make it to the set when they are needed. Also called the second AD, this person helps the AD as needed.

Whereas the AD is in charge of the call sheet, the second AD creates the call sheet. This document details the times actors are picked up, when they need to be in makeup, and when they have to be on set. Director Sidney Lumet refers to the call sheet as the filmmaker's bible. It also lists the scenes being shot that day, and the kind of setting for each scene. It is the guide for the day's shooting, both for cast and crew, so the person creating it must know what they are doing.

The second AD also makes sure everyone knows their call time, and that they are ready for it. Like the AD, this position requires good organization, attention to detail, and time management.

Third Assistant Director

No film or TV show looks real without the background extras and activity. The third AD is responsible for coordinating and preparing the extras, or the people hired to fill in the background to create realistic environments, and sometimes even directing them on what they should be doing in the background. He or she may also need to keep the public off the set or out of the background.

Director of Photography/ Cinematographer

Usually shortened to DOP or DP, the director of photography, or cinematographer, is often a main creative conspirator with the director. Together, they create the look of the story being shot and ensure that the actors' blocking, which is the movements that the actors do during a scene, works. This person also oversees the camera and lighting crew.

Before shooting starts, they read the screenplay so they can develop the film or TV show's style with the director, as well as create a list of equipment needed to shoot the story. For films with smaller crews, the DOP might also run the camera.

Some directors like to work with the same DOP and become long-term creative partners. Janusz Kaminski is known as Steven Spielberg's cinematographer and has worked with him on many films, including *Schindler's List*, *War Horse*, and *Lincoln*. Other directors might pick their DOP depending on the film they are making.

Production Assistant/Runner

This role isn't one that directs; however, they support the other assistant directors and are key to a smooth-running set. A production assistant (also called a PA, runner, or gofer) will do a variety of tasks, including run errands, give messages, organize the props for a shoot, provide snacks and drinks for the cast and crew, and any other tasks given to them.

So what's the benefit of being a movie or television gofer? The PA is the entry-level position where people intending to become directors, producers, or other film professionals often start. It provides a great vantage point to learn from watching great directors and to see if directing is really what they want to do. In fact, this is the position most cited as the first step into the movie business.

Many young people can gain directing experience while in school. These students are shooting a film in New York City.

CHAPTER THREE

How Do You Get Involved Now?

Becoming a director doesn't have to happen after college or film school or as an older adult. Those who want to take on the challenge and fun of directing can start building the knowledge and confidence they need in high school.

Directing Your Future

Successful director James Cameron has something to say about directing:

> Pick up a camera. Shoot something. No matter how small, no matter how cheesy, no matter whether your friends and your sister star in it. Put your name on it as director ... Now you're a director. Everything after that, you're just negotiating your budget and your fee.

While this advice seems smart-alecky, it's true. Cameron picked up a camera in his early teens and began his directing career. Considering how well he has done, it's probably good advice. He's really just telling you to go for it and believe in yourself.

Create Videos and Short Films

When successful directors give advice to young people who want to follow in their career footprints, they pretty much always say one thing: make movies or videos.

Even if the videos are five minutes long, make them. Even if it's with your cell phone or your grandpa's old video recorder, make them. Whether it's a stop-motion film using LEGO figures or you filming your best friends in the backyard, make them.

Why do the pros say this? If you are passionate about something, you should find a way to do it—and this is a trait that directors need. On top of that, too many people think they want to be directors and follow that dream for a long time before getting a chance to do it. When they finally get their chance, they discover that they hate it. By making as many short films (called "shorts") as possible, you will discover whether you really enjoy the work of being a director or might prefer a different film-related career—or an entirely different career.

Plus, short films make great learning experiences. You may think yours will turn out silly or crude, but working through the process of creating a story, planning your shoot, sourcing the items you need, directing actors in a scene (even if they are friends with no acting experience), and editing what you shoot will only help you develop your style and your sense of storytelling. It is little wonder that many directors film their first story in their teenage years, not as adults.

Portfolios and Demo Reels

The bonus of doing this work is that it will help you build a portfolio or a demo reel. A portfolio is a collection of several of your best pieces of video and related work to use when applying to colleges or to jobs in film and television. This is often used to apply to college film programs.

Requirements for portfolios vary from school to school but could include five to fifteen minutes of video, which could be one video or parts of several videos. Today, schools may want portfolios sent via DVD, web links, or an online app such as SlideRoom. Other elements that may be requested include three to ten pages of a film script or short story that highlights storytelling ability, ten to fifteen images arranged

Modern technology makes it easier than ever to shoot and edit a film. Today, almost anyone can try his or her hand at directing and editing.

to tell a story like a storyboard, and other work such as photography, scholarly work, and documents that prove participation as an actor or director.

A demo reel, sometimes called a show reel, is used to apply for film and television jobs. It is similar in that it should highlight a director's best work, but it often doesn't include the written samples or other materials that might be included in a portfolio. The reel includes the best shots or scenes from a director's work, though sometimes a short film (less than ten minutes long) makes a bigger impression than a sampling of different shots. Demo reels usually include a cover letter and résumé.

DIY Effects and Props

The next logical step after starting to make your own films is to take them to the next level! Turn to YouTube or Pinterest, and you can find hundreds of how-to videos and articles showing you how to create makeup effects and props too. Another source for this information is the local library. See if yours has any books on how to make special effects or stagecraft.

Here are some examples of things you can learn to do on a basic level:

- Make an actor look older or younger with makeup

- Create fake scars

- Mix up some fake blood with kitchen supplies

- Give glass bottles an old, distressed look. Perfect for portraying potion bottles or old-fashioned medicine bottles

- Make fake seaweed from trash bags, useful for shooting your rendition of *The Little Mermaid* or *Swamp Thing*

- Create a mannequin (or a monster model) from paper bags, wallpaper paste, and tape

- Make tombstones out of foam

- Sculpt fake rocks from chicken wire, paper towels, plaster, and paint. Perfect for filming explosions without hurting your cast

- Film objects to look animated without animatronics

Choose a couple effects and practice them. Then, add these effects to a short film. Or just create a short video clip featuring the effect so you can see how it looks onscreen. Try a couple more effects and apply them. Even if these tricks don't look perfect, they are bound to add more fun to filming, and they will give you an understanding of the challenges that art directors, makeup, and effects artists face every day.

When it comes to props, set pieces, and costumes, sometimes it's about being resourceful rather than creating things from scratch. Can you find old furniture or household items that can be repurposed for your set? How about old clothes? Can they be altered, shortened, or dyed to make them fit your story? Try your hand at making a few things to add some realism to your next shoot.

Drama and Stagecraft

While acting is not the same thing as directing, drama and theater classes are recommended for those wanting to sit in the director's chair. Even if you never become a great actor, the experience gives you something that you will need in abundance as a director: the actor's perspective. This not only helps you to communicate with the cast without annoying them but also will show you how actors work and how to motivate them.

Some drama classes discuss the different acting methods, but if they don't, consider researching them on your own. They are important to understand

These high school students rehearse on stage. Drama and stagecraft activities are great learning experiences for up-and-coming filmmakers.

because they will help you communicate better with your cast members.

Stagecraft classes and working behind the curtains of a play prove helpful as well. As a director, you must have some knowledge of how the departments of a film or television production work in order to communicate your vision without misunderstandings. Building sets, running the lightboard, or putting together costumes gives you an understanding of how the different teams all support the goal of amazing storytelling. This can also help you relate to technical and design members on a shoot and create a better working relationship with them.

Other School Activities

While drama might be the obvious choice among the school activities for a future director, there are many others that build the skills and strengths needed. There may be a film club or video club in your school or community. Get involved in those opportunities if you can (or start a club yourself). However, if your school offers more traditional activities, don't worry. Those can help you too.

When looking at the skills a director needs— creativity, ability to meet deadlines, leadership, teamwork, decision-making, and confidence—it's easy to see that anything that requires you to develop these will help, even if they aren't related to theater or filmmaking. Participating in school publications or TV channels will boost all those skills or traits by requiring you to work with others, interview sources, write articles, take photos or video footage, meet deadlines, and make quick decisions. Forensics/debate teams build confidence, leadership, and quick thinking. Even participating in athletics teams will help you develop a sense of teamwork and confidence.

Look to Your Community

It's easy to think you are out of luck if your school doesn't offer many opportunities. However, that's not always true. You simply might need to look a little further. Most communities have organizations that produce plays or musicals for the public. Some will even offer summer workshops teaching acting and other theater skills. Participating in these provides the same chance to develop or expand your skills as does a school production, if not more. You will also learn to work with people of different ages and benefit from experienced performers.

Nothing like that in your town? Why not write and direct a play for your church, scout troop, or town festival? You are limited only by your imagination and determination.

Watch Movies with a Fresh Eye (or Ear)

Yes, it's assumed that if you are interested in becoming a director, you enjoy watching movies and shows. Now, you should watch them in a different way than a casual viewer would. After you've seen a movie once, watch it again and look for the key elements of storytelling, how the plot progresses, where special effects are used, and so on.

To learn how films work visually, watch a movie with the sound turned off. This also helps you learn how camera shots are used. Or listen to a movie while keeping your eyes closed. This teaches you how important dialogue, sound effects, and the musical score are to the viewer.

If you watch on DVD or Blu-ray, there are usually special features, including the film or show with commentary from the writers, directors, actors, and producers. Watching this commentary version can help you understand why certain choices were made for the story. This can give you insight for how to make your own stories more dramatic and how to shoot them better.

Educate Yourself

Between now and film school (if you even choose to go to film school—more on that later), giving yourself an informal education is a good idea. Read books

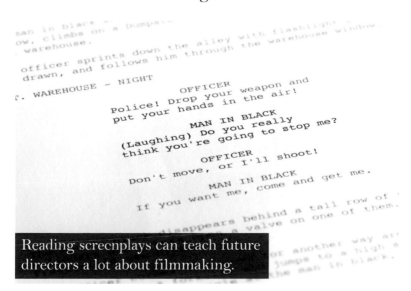

Reading screenplays can teach future directors a lot about filmmaking.

on how to make movies and videos or biographies about directors. Find articles interviewing directors or other film professionals. You can learn a lot from how other people made their way into the business. There are also YouTube channels, such as RocketJump Film School, and podcasts, such as *No Film School*, that provide a ton of useful information for amateur filmmakers plus interviews with experienced film and television directors.

Find and read screenplays. Seeing how movies are written can only help you be better prepared for directing. You can see firsthand how much information in a screenplay is for the director and how much is pure dialogue. Then, you can watch the film and see how a director interpreted the script. Then think about what you would have done differently.

On rare occasions, a screenplay is published as a book, such as *Fantastic Beasts and Where to Find Them*, but there are many screenplays available online for free at sites such as Script Reader Pro and Screenplays for You. Take advantage of as many free resources as you can.

Understanding the Stages of Production

Though it's easy to focus on the director's role during filming, they have a lot of work to do during all stages of production. Let's look at some of the key jobs of each stage.

Preproduction

This could start when a director gets an idea for a film and decides to develop the story on his or her own. It could be when a director gets a call from his or her agent saying that there is a studio with a script that might interest him or her. However it starts, it's the beginning of a year's journey (or longer) that will challenge the director.

During this stage, which is the planning and preparation before any filming starts, a director does research on the film's subject and then helps with casting, choosing shots, filming locations, and developing a style and themes. He or she may even assist in finding money for the project. This is a lot of work for a director before shooting begins, but it is important work. Research and preparation gives the director the background and insight to make quick decisions later in production—decisions that aren't

The girl with the red coat in *Schindler's List* stood out as a symbol due to the style of the film.

made on a whim. These steps ensure that the movie is cohesive and has some depth. For example, style may not always be obvious to a viewer, but many directors use style and themes to add more meaning to the story.

One example of style choices and its effect on the film is Steven Spielberg's *Schindler's List*. This Oscar-winning film was shot in black and white even though it was made well into the era of color film. Why did Spielberg do this? Critics have examined this question quite a bit over the years.

The film is about the treatment of the Jews in Nazi-occupied Poland during World War II, and some think shooting in black and white helped take the modern viewer back in time. This effect made the movie resemble the newsreels from World War II, adding realism to the tragic events. There were two times when Spielberg did add color to the film, however: for Shabbat candles and for the red coat of a young Jewish girl. This put more emphasis on these two objects, which were two key symbols of the film, representing the Jewish faith and innocence.

Production

With all the preplanning done, it's time for a director to get their hands dirty! OK, not literally, but the production stage is when the film or show is actually shot, and the director must work diligently to keep the shooting on schedule and to provide the actors with feedback about their performances.

Production is the time when a director's leadership and quick decision making is key to staying on schedule and on budget. What does the shooting process look like? It is summed up as: block, light, rehearse, and shoot.

What is blocking? It is how the director, director of photography, and others plan for the actors to move during a scene. This is usually drawn on paper before shooting, but the blocking rehearsal with the actors may reveal that the movement is awkward or doesn't fit the lighting. Some changes to the blocking may be needed to solve these problems.

The production crew that lights the set comes in next and positions the lights in the way needed for the blocking and to limit the number of equipment changes as much as possible. What does "equipment changes" mean? Well, as actors move on the set, the angle of the lights and cameras may need to change to catch their performance. It wastes time to move lights

After an on-set rehearsal, comedian Jon Stewart reviews script rewrites.

and cameras more than is absolutely necessary, so the crew tries to minimize this through careful planning.

The regular rehearsal is next and, in many productions, everyone who needs to see where the action takes place on the set is there to prepare for their part of the filming.

Finally, the shoot begins and, with any luck, all the preparations add up to the director capturing amazing performances on film. This process occurs daily during production, but the director must focus on working with the actors and technical people to get the best results possible while still handling questions from all directions. Needless to say, this is a tough but rewarding job.

The Call Sheet: The Director's Bible

Sidney Lumet, who directed classics such as *Network* and *The Verdict*, said the call sheet was the filmmaker's bible, and he was right. The call sheet is the schedule of everything that needs to happen on the day of a shoot, including when the actors arrive, go to makeup, and appear on set; what scenes are being shot that day and with which characters; and whether each scene is an interior or exterior shot.

Near the end of filming on any given day, the production office sends the director a draft of the next day's call sheet. If the director didn't get all the shots that were scheduled for that day, he or she will have to add them to the next day's call sheet and send it back to be finalized. Running behind on a regular basis can make a production schedule get off track.

In 1951, director Roberto Rossellini works on
a filming schedule, referred to as a call sheet.
This keeps shooting on track. His wife, actress
Ingrid Bergman, peers over his shoulder.

JAMES CAMERON: FROM COLLEGE DROPOUT TO MOVIE MASTER

Not all directors go to film school. One of Hollywood's most successful directors didn't. In fact, he didn't even finish college.

Canadian James Cameron had an early fascination with science fiction and fantasy. Though he considered a film career in his youth, he struggled to find a path that balanced his love of art and science. He majored in physics at Fullerton College in California; however, he switched to English when he didn't excel in calculus.

Cameron dropped out of college in 1974 and worked several jobs while attending to creative projects. He combed the University of Southern California's library for student papers on filmmaking. He photocopied them, providing himself with a free film education. Cameron was hired to build spaceship models for New World Pictures, where he was promoted to the Front Screen Projection Department and then to art director in just weeks. On his second film, Cameron made an impression as the second unit director.

His first shot at directing came for *Piranha Part II* in 1981, but he was fired after five days. While in Italy to see the film's rough cut, which is the first edited version of a film that doesn't have all the editing done or the soundtrack added to it yet, Cameron was sick and dreamed of a chrome torso emerging from an explosion. He returned home, broke, but stayed

with a friend while writing the treatment, or a short document that highlights the major parts of the film before the screenplay is written, for what became *The Terminator.* In 1982, he and Gale Anne Hurd teamed up and secured financing for the film, which was ultimately released in 1984.

Cameron wrote scripts for the *Alien* and *Rambo* sequels at the same time. *The Terminator* and *Aliens*, which he also directed, became box office hits and launched his career. He went on to direct *Titanic* and *Avatar*, two of the highest-grossing movies in history.

The Language of Shooting

A huge part of directing and having the director of photography and others understand what you want is knowing the names of different styles of shots. Below are the most common and useful camera shots, but there are many more you could learn:

In this scene from the movie *Black Panther*, we see use of the medium shot. This is the most common shot.

medium shot This type of shot is used the most, especially when there is dialogue back and forth between characters. The medium shot shows the character from head to waist.

long shot/wide shot This shows the character far enough away to show their whole body plus some of the setting, yet close enough to show some details about the character.

establishing shot Many television shows and films start with a really wide shot showing the setting of the story. This is called the establishing shot because it shows where the character is and sometimes even sets the tone of the story.

close-up This shot focuses tightly in on a character, usually the face, although hands or feet are also common depending on what's being depicted. When focused on the face, the close-up is often used to show emotion.

extreme close-up Have you seen footage of the actor Clint Eastwood in a Western film where almost the entire frame is his eyes squinting against the sun? That would be a classic example of the extreme close-up.

pan When the camera pivots to shoot a sweeping horizontal shot without moving the camera body, this is called panning. This is often used to follow a character or to show distance.

tilt Take the panning shot and change it from horizontal to vertical in movement and you have a tilt shot. This is used to show something or someone from top to bottom by tilting the camera. You might see this used when a character has made a dramatic change or when showing the sky and moving to the action on the ground.

50/50 Two characters are in an argument, face-to-face, toe-to-toe, or perhaps a romantic duo edges in for a kiss. Both examples have the basic element of the 50/50, which is two subjects facing each other in the frame. The examples also show what this shot is good at: building tension.

tracking If a camera moves along with the character, keeping him or her in frame as he or she moves through the environment, that is called a tracking shot. To do this smoothly, a camera dolly, which is a rolling platform for the camera, or a Steadicam, which is a stabilization device that lets someone carry a camera and keep it steady, is usually needed.

over-the-shoulders This involves shooting over one character's shoulder while focusing on the face of another character.

point of view This is simply a shot that shows what the character is looking at. It could be a sweeping vista of a mountain range to establish the character's awe at a natural landscape, or a mess of papers the character is searching through, looking for a clue to a mystery.

A film crew works on a tracking shot, where the camera moves with the subject.

Postproduction

When the shooting is complete and the last "Cut!" has been called, it's time for the polishing and digital magic to happen. Usually, directors aren't as hands on during this stage, but they still supervise the processes of editing (also called cutting) the shots together into a cohesive story. Then comes color correction to create professional-looking footage and adding sound and visual effects.

Some directors do choose to dig into film editing or other parts of postproduction—or even the production itself—if they have the skill set to make it work. For example, James Cameron is known to do screenwriting, art production (that's actually where he started his film career), and editing.

Though it's good to understand all the departments that make a film, it's also good to know when to let professionals do their thing and to take their advice so your story is the best it can be.

Directing in TV

Thus far, we have looked at how directors work in general but with a little more emphasis on movie directors. Now let's look closer at television production and discuss how it differs from film directing.

Fans who follow the news of their favorite television series often hear the term "showrunner" (another name for the executive producer), especially when a show gets a new one. Controversial changes to this position in shows like Marvel's *Daredevil* series on Netflix, *The Walking Dead,* and *Community* made a big splash in entertainment news when they happened.

This is for a good reason. Unlike movies where the director is the creative leader, the showrunner is the creative authority on most television shows. The show's other producers and writers may have influence in molding the show. Consequently, meetings with the showrunner, writers, director, and assistant director to discuss tone and intention for an episode are important to a television director's work. So, if the director isn't the creative leader for a television show, what are they?

Directors in television may not have the control that they do in movies, but they are still the magicians that pull together all the disciplines and bring the vision to life. Because directors are usually hired by episode rather than by season, they have the added challenge of blending what they film into an existing style for the show.

An advantage to television directing is that you have an experienced cast and crew who already have a good understanding of the show's style and direction. Plus, television is often where directors get their feet wet before landing a feature film.

Directors may not direct more than a handful of episodes for a single show, unless they are a favorite director of a long-running show. Working in television requires you to hit the ground running since episodes are on a tight programming schedule, with shooting taking six to eight days. For this pace, you must make more compromises and focus your best efforts on the episode's important scenes instead of trying to make them all perfect or unique.

While many movie directors get their start in television while biding their time for a shot at a feature film, some feature filmmakers are turning to television and finding fertile ground for their stories.

Movie directors such as Guillermo del Toro, Jane Campion, and Spike Lee are creating short television series, such as *The Strain, Top of the Lake*, and *She's Gotta Have It,* that give directors more creative control and bring film production quality to the television format. Some newcomers, such as Matt and Ross Duffer with their hit show *Stranger Things*, are finding the short TV series as a way to kick-start a career while maintaining control of their projects.

Being a director means stress, problem-solving, and working with all departments. It's a tough but rewarding job.

CHAPTER FOUR

Setbacks and Challenges Faced

Every job has its ups and downs, and directing is no different. While a director leads with creativity and skills, there are some things that can wear down even the cheeriest of people. There are situations that every director must be prepared for, and mistakes that most directors make at some point in their career.

Communication Is Key

Communication is an important skill for directors to have. A movie is the art of communicating meaning and emotion to the audience, so it's no surprise that movies require a ton of it during production to make that happen.

Directors are not lone visionaries. They are the head of a creative team that is composed of people with very different skills and personalities. Directors often collaborate closely with the director of photography to achieve the desired look and impact of a story. Actors are also key partners for the director. Though actors are seen as extroverts, some are actually introverted and shy—even famous actors like Johnny Depp and Jessica Chastain have said they are shy. A director must work closely with actors to get the best results for the film or TV show. Directors also might be called on to talk to film investors. On top of all that, they might be training a new assistant director. It requires a special person to balance all these different communication needs.

Below are some methods directors use to improve communication with the cast and crew.

Knowing the Different Acting Methods

Many will suggest that the relationship between director and actor is the most important one on set. Whether or not that is true, the communication between the two is key to getting a great performance. A director needs to understand an actor and learn how to communicate with each one. Some are very sensitive and cannot deal with curtness or harshness. Some actors require being shaken up and pushed to deliver a strong performance. Some actors are shy and introverted, while others are the life of the party.

One key directors use to communicate and work with actors is knowing what acting method they use. Understanding that an actor uses method acting instead of classical acting helps a director get what he or she needs from the actor's performance. After all, weak or confused performances take away from the story the director wants to tell. A director might discover that some actors work outside an established

Daniel Day-Lewis, a method actor, portrayed Abraham Lincoln by utilizing some unusual techniques.

system. Sidney Lumet said that British actor Ralph Richardson created his own system using musical metaphors, and he learned to direct Richardson using those metaphors.

The following is an overview of common acting techniques.

Classical

This is the traditional style of acting that mixes several theories, including voice, expression of the body, improvisation, external stimuli, analyzing scripts, personalizing, and more. These actors focus on physically acting the role while staying true to the script. They may carefully explore the subtext of a story and use their own memories and imagination to help them connect to a character, but they will focus on getting the lines and action right first.

Stanislavski's System

This method also encourages the use of emotional memory for performances. To grasp the character, actors are also encouraged to ask key questions such as "Who am I?" and "How will I get what I want?" The point of this system is to make acting more realistic. The technique was developed by Russian actor and director Konstantin Stanislavski. He was the first person in Western culture to suggest actors go beyond the classical acting method.

Method

Sometimes actors who use method acting make headlines with their strange behavior, but it feeds their performance. This method relies on the actor using powerful emotions to fuel their performance, often calling on their own joyous or painful memories to do so. Method actors also try to dig deeply into what their character experiences, to the point of causing themselves physical pain. They avoid overanalyzing their performances.

An actor notorious for his use of method acting is Daniel Day-Lewis. He immerses himself into a character so completely that he might not come out of character for months. When shooting *The Last of the Mohicans*, he learned how to build a canoe and trap animals. When taking on the title role in *Lincoln*, Lewis reportedly insisted that cast and crew—even director Steven Spielberg—call him Mr. Lincoln. The British native would not talk to anyone with a British accent during filming because he was afraid it would disrupt his ability to maintain an appropriate accent for Abraham Lincoln.

Practical Aesthetics

Though it can seem similar to method acting, practical aesthetics focuses more on script and performance analysis. This system also likes to connect the character's progressions with essential actions, or actions that represent the character's goal and personality.

There are many more techniques to explore and learn, and many directors learn as much as possible to understand what motivates actors, even if they don't really care how the performance is achieved.

Learning to Ask for Money

When people think of a director, they think of a creative person who is a leader. They think of someone with vision and passion. They probably don't think of someone who can balance a budget and find money for filming, but that's part of the job too.

Sometimes a director is sought out by a studio and given a generous budget to start with, especially after they've achieved some fame, such as Christopher Nolan or Guillermo del Toro. However, most often, lesser-known directors have to make pitches to get funding for a production they are working on. He or she may have to officially present in front of a group or have a lunch meeting with people who care more about numbers than vision. As making movies is a bit of a gamble financially, he or she needs to be persuasive.

This, of course, is another case of needing communication but with the addition of having to be compelling and personable in order to convince those with funds to spend them on an entertainment venture. This has become more difficult in the last decade as studios are less likely to spend money on a production if it isn't geared toward box office success, an Oscar award, or television ratings. For many smaller independent films, crowd funding has become common practice.

If a studio won't pay attention to the story, a director must look for creative financing. By "creative," that doesn't mean maxing out personal credit cards (though some filmmakers have done that). Sometimes, a filmmaker can rely on friends and family. Rian Johnson, who wrote and directed *Star Wars: The Last Jedi* and *Looper*, spent more than six years finding money to start shooting his debut movie, *Brick*. He eventually tightened the budget, and his family invested almost half of the amount he would need to shoot the film.

Below are some different ways that directors finance their films.

Equity

Equity is simply individuals or groups that choose to invest their own money into a project. This sounds like a dream, but with any investment comes paid dividends, or rather, they will own a stake in the project. So when the film is released, the investors must be paid back, plus interest, before the director sees any of the profit.

Films or television shows are rarely the business of these investors, so filmmakers approaching anyone outside of entertainment have to be ready to explain the costs and benefits in terms the everyday person can understand, not studio executives or producers. The plus side to this is many people are excited to support an artistic project and be part of it.

One never knows what people or groups might want to finance a project. It could be the director's grandparents or a group of businesspeople. James Cameron, director of *Avatar* and *Titanic*, was financed for his first film by a group of dentists!

Presales Agreements

If a film project is promising, film distributors will sometimes make presales agreements with the filmmakers. These are when the distributor believes they will make money from the film if they distribute it, so they allow the director to take out a loan using the agreement as collateral. When the film is complete, the loan must be paid back before the director makes any money.

Crowdfunding

Most people today have heard of crowdfunding via Kickstarter, Indiegogo, and other platforms. Basically, you ask for pledges from anyone online who might be interested. This works well for some projects, including films, but donors are usually promised something for donating after the project is completed. A DVD signed by the cast or an acknowledgement in the credits would be basic pledge gifts.

Mythica, a five-movie independent series steeped in fantasy, was partially funded through crowdfunding. This campaign's advantage was that it had an existing fan base of people who love fantasy and Dungeons & Dragons–style stories. On top of that, the series featured actor Kevin Sorbo (*Hercules* and *Andromeda*) and voice actor Matthew Mercer (*Final Fantasy* video games and *Critical Role*), who were already known names in entertainment. By targeting these fans, the movie producers were able to secure financing to finish the first three movies and then continue to produce the fourth and fifth movies.

Deferrals

Deferrals are contracts that ask that everyone work on the film without pay. Instead, they will receive a percentage of the film's profit. This requires trust between the cast and crew and the director and producer, and sometimes deferrals are not paid as promised. This is also tricky if the film doesn't fare well and no one is compensated for their work.

All of these methods require someone to share their vision with other people, many of whom will be outside of entertainment. They require a polished presentation, whether it's at a meeting with financiers or on a crowdfunding site appealing to someone across the country, and the ability to make others enthusiastic about a product.

Asking for money is one thing, but managing it is quite another. Directors must take charge of ensuring that the costs of the production—from the camera equipment and sets to the actors' salaries and the cost of feeding a crew—stays within the production's means. This requires the director to know how much is being spent in all departments and how much money will be required to finish production and postproduction.

Getting Technical

If it is important to learn to communicate with a cast, it's also true that communicating with the crew and other film professionals is vital. Learning these technical aspects or asking questions about them is something directors find helpful. When directing his first feature film, *American Beauty*, Sam Mendes realized after looking at some of the first few scenes that he'd made poor decisions on shots, costumes, and more. This taught him to ask questions about technical matters he didn't understand. It's a good thing he learned this lesson quickly, as the film went on to win five Academy Awards in 2000, including for Best Director.

Many directors also do some screenwriting, especially if they came up with the story concept that they want to shoot. Whether or not a director is also a writer, it is helpful to understand how much work a writer puts into a screenplay, as well as the process of developing a good story. It isn't unusual for screenwriters to be brought in for certain parts of preproduction and production, so it's a good idea to discover the keys to working with them.

Art production, makeup, and wardrobe are departments that must work well together to create a cohesive look for a set. They handle the complexities of creating lifelike sets and props and unusual makeup effects that age, disfigure, or otherwise alter the appearance of an actor. They are both technicians and artists. Being able to describe what looks a director wants to achieve—and understanding what's possible—can help keep a set production rolling smoothly.

The director and director of photography work closely together. Even if they choose not to go behind the camera, directors should understand how cameras work and how different shots can be achieved. Speaking in the DOP's shorthand keeps the close working relationship functional and productive.

Film editing is another area many directors say is important to have some experience in, even if they don't do final editing. When a film or show is cut, the director views the rough cut and discusses with the film editor how to fine-tune and provide continuity through the film. If directors work closely with the DOP in production, they work just as closely with the film editor in postproduction.

All of these and many other specialists have their own terminology for what they do, and it benefits a filmmaker to learn it in order to communicate efficiently in all stages of production.

Challenges to Face, Not Fear

Aside from communication issues, there are many things that can turn directing from a dream job into a disappointment. They can all be overcome or managed, but directors need to be prepared to handle the less glamorous aspects of the job.

Considering Film School

Finding a way to the director's chair can seem straightforward: go to film school, graduate from film school, and become a big-time movie director. This is far from reality. Film school may sound like the perfect idea for a future director, but it is just one way to achieve the goal.

There are many amazing directors who went to film school, such as Martin Scorsese, George Lucas, and Patty Jenkins. There are also many who did not: Kevin Smith, Steven Spielberg, Peter Jackson, Greta Gerwig, and even Alfred Hitchcock. Attending film school is no guarantee that someone will become a director, and it is an expensive way to aim for the job. Even with film school, a future director needs drive, skills, good film examples, good contacts, and luck.

While attending film school is one way people develop skills and portfolio pieces while meeting experienced professionals or other students to collaborate with, this is not the only way to achieve the goal.

With digital technology, it is easier (and cheaper) than ever to create a film or video. Steven Soderbergh, director of *Erin Brockovich* and *Traffic*, shot his 2018 film *Unsane* completely with an iPhone. With inexpensive digital cameras that shoot video and smartphones with higher-resolution video, more people are becoming independent filmmakers without breaking the bank.

Many develop shorts during this learning process and use them in a portfolio or film reel. While this is unlikely to get someone the director's job on a major film or TV show, it has frequently been the way people get in the door as a production assistant or another entry-level position. Many directors start out in similar roles and work their way up. Other people begin by writing screenplays or learning to be a cinematographer and change into the director's role later.

When it comes to deciding whether or not to go to film school, future filmmakers often consider their learning style and personality. If they prefer an academic setting with structure, film school is a good fit. If hands-on and experience-based learning is more their style, creating shorts and film treatments while getting their foot in the door of the film industry as a gofer or other entry-level position is a better option.

More Than One Way to Be a Director

Directing in film is a tough business, and some people might be excellent at a lot of the tasks that a director handles but not every aspect of the job. Being away from home for weeks or months can be very difficult, even more so if the director has a family. Add in the building pressure—the runaway train momentum that

People can learn, develop, and apply directing skills while in high school and, later, film school.

a movie shoot when too and it can be too stressful for otherwise great filmmakers.

But keep in mind that making movies isn't the only way to direct. There are many other outlets for directing that are less time consuming and often less stressful. Television shows are a great example. Typical shows often hire numerous directors throughout a season, so it spreads out the workload. A single episode of TV usually takes seven working days to shoot, plus preproduction and postproduction time. All total, being hired to direct an episode wouldn't require more than three or four weeks.

Documentaries are another option, and they vary quite a bit in length of time to shoot. They could take just a few weeks or much longer. The documentary subject often dictates how much shooting is required. Most of these types of films require much more research in preproduction, but research can often be done at home.

Commercials and music videos are two other areas where directors build their portfolio and pay the bills. These are very different mediums than TV or films, but they are fast paced and provide a creative outlet. The down side to some of these directing jobs is that because they are shorter, a director has to look for work more frequently.

Handling Egos and Feuds

One of the complexities that directors deal with is the personalities and conflicts of the cast. Some actors have very specific requests that must be met before they will agree to work on a film. A set of such requests is called a rider. Many riders focus on comforts such as transportation or a private bathroom. While most beginning actors have food requests, some of the stranger demands by stars include not having any extras look them in the eye or insisting that no gear with a certain sports logo be on set. Some stars' riders require items that inflate the production's budget by $100,000 or more!

Beyond these demands, some actors have quirky personalities and many, which they often admit to, are rather sensitive. Other times, actors who must have chemistry on screen simply don't like each other in reality. *X-Files* actors David Duchovny and Gillian Anderson have both been straightforward about their dislike of one another and bad attitudes while filming the popular sci-fi show. Though they patched things up before they returned to their iconic roles in 2016, there were times in the past when they wouldn't speak to each other except when shooting. Sometimes the personality of an actor actually makes the crew dislike them to the point that a feud starts there.

The director must be able to handle these demands, personalities, and conflicts. Director Danny Boyle elaborates on this part of directing: "People who've never done it imagine that it's some act, like painting a Picasso from a blank canvas, but it's not like that. Directing is mostly about handling people's egos, vulnerabilities, and moods."

Again, communication is often the key to eliminating or managing these problems, but directors must also be flexible in dealing with personalities while maintaining creative control of the filming. They must know when to intervene during a dispute and when to let people work it out on their own.

A future filmmaker can start learning how to work through these situations by participating in school or community plays, where many of the same personality conflicts can appear, or doing any activity that requires teamwork. Shooting short videos or movies with friends can also help someone practice this skill.

Managing Stress and Long Hours

Stress goes hand-in-hand with filmmaking. Take a look at a typical schedule: preproduction can take up to four months, production (shooting) averages ten to twelve weeks, and postproduction can take six months. That's if nothing big happens to derail the plans.

During shooting, many different teams must work together on schedule to keep things running smoothly. The weather might postpone an outdoor shoot. Shooting locations might be difficult to book. Directors might have to shoot in extremely hot temperatures or in cold rain. They work long hours: after a day of shooting, they still have to watch the footage of what was shot on the previous day, called dailies, and ensure things are in order for the next day of shooting. They are the boss and have to maintain their own drive for the story while handling dozens of questions and interruptions. Clearly, this is no easy job.

Even after years of acting, actress Angelina Jolie admitted to having a breakdown from the stress of directing her first film, *In the Land of Blood and Honey*. Yet she picked herself up and finished it. Celebrated director Martin Scorsese, who has made more than sixty movies, said that he feels physically sick every time he views a rough cut of one of his films.

Learning to deal with stress will come in handy for anyone wanting to take on the director's job. For some directors, having a very structured day is helpful. Sidney Lumet would take naps during the lunch break to stay fresh. Relaxation techniques, such as deep belly breathing, can help.

Stay focused on the goal and block out unnecessary distractions, and understand that stress helps push creativity. Without pressure, people often remain in stasis. Filmmakers stay focused and confident, and delegate tasks to assistant and second assistant directors as needed. They learn to breathe, and then they make their story.

Overcoming Racial and Gender Bias

Sad as it is to admit, there is still some bias in filmmaking and television. However, there have been strides made in recent years. In 2017, the three top-grossing films all featured female-led stories, but only one of those, *Wonder Woman*, was directed by a woman, Patty Jenkins. *Black Panther* became a huge hit in 2018 and featured both a mostly black cast as well as a black director, Ryan Coogler. A black woman, Ava DuVernay, directed another 2018 major film, *A Wrinkle in Time*. Despite these positive signs, bias against female directors and directors of color remains a roadblock to many creative people.

In 2014, scandal broke out when a hacker group made public confidential records from Sony Pictures. Among other things, it revealed that women in Hollywood are paid far less than their male counterparts, even established stars that are household names. And behind the camera, it can get worse. Among the highest-grossing films from 2002 to 2014, the male-to-female director ratio was 23 to 1. Considering that women make up half of film school graduates, this doesn't add up.

The same study that looked at this asked producers and studio executives why they didn't hire more women. Here are some of their reasons:

- Women want to make niche films and not ones that appeal to a broader audience.

- Women cannot handle large crews or technical aspects of production.

- 25 percent said they didn't think women wanted to direct studio films (though 44 percent of female directors said that they did want to).

Another complaint found among female directors is that they are often "babysat" by producers. When a director is to handle a meeting on their own, the producer will often insist on attending if the director is a woman. The level of trust is higher with male directors.

In 2016, the Oscars were the target of black actors and film professionals when, for the second year in a row, there were no black actors nominated for an award despite several powerful performances that year. Less than 7 percent of Hollywood films have black directors. Latino and Asian directors fare no better.

This is clearly not representative of the diverse world that we all live in, but it will take work to change. Some say the best way for a minority director to break through is via film festivals. Though they are competitive, they are more representative. For example, the male-to-female director ratio for festival films is 3 to 1. By getting noticed at one of hundreds of film festivals, such as Sundance, Cannes, or a regional festival, it can help a director connect with producers who might hire them for a studio film.

Minority filmmakers say to learn as much as possible and to be confident in that knowledge. Stand up for yourself and prove that you can do the job. Also, minority directors need to help each other. Often, directors are hired because of who they know—and who they know is often a reflection of themselves. As there aren't many minority directors at work in Hollywood, it can be difficult to rely on who you know to help, so it is even more important for women and directors of color to connect with and support each other.

There Will Be Ups and Downs

Very few directors make nothing but amazing box office hits; some movies will be excellent, some movies will be OK, and some will be worse. A look at the career of M. Night Shyamalan, who came to achieve huge successes with *The Sixth Sense, Unbreakable*, and *Signs*, proves the point. While he was initially known for creating exciting, new ideas for audiences, soon people caught on to Shyamalan's use of dramatic twists and tired of it. Since that time, his movies have not seen the same acclaim or monetary success.

While Shyamalan's descent is notable due to his incredible heights achieved, it is not unusual for directors to have to rebuild after one or two poor releases. Tom Holland, director of horror classics *Child's Play* and *Fright Night*, sums it up: "The problem isn't being successful, the problem is staying successful. You think that being successful is going to solve all your problems, and it doesn't. You're still you. I still try all the time. I still fail all the time."

Filmmakers are prepared for this rollercoaster ride and are flexible and keep learning about storytelling in new ways. Collaborating with others helps push a director out of his or her comfort zone and sharpen his or her abilities. Some find ways to nurture creativity, such as through travel or taking on new hobbies, and working on unique and fresh stories can keep someone innovative and inspired.

WONDER WOMAN'S LONG ROAD TO THE BIG SCREEN

Perseverance is a quality needed by any moviemaker. The 2017 box office hit *Wonder Woman* was one film that required patience and perseverance.

The iconic DC Comics character was created in 1941 but did not come to television until 1974. It took another forty-three years to see the character headline a movie. By comparison, Superman was created in 1938 and headlined a film just fourteen years later.

Some say that Wonder Woman's mythology was too complex for filmmakers to tackle, but a Wonder Woman movie was hinted at in 1996, 1999, and 2005, all connected to different directors. In 2004 and 2005, the films *Catwoman* and *Elektra* both failed to draw audiences. According to *Catwoman*'s director, people didn't want to see a female lead in a superhero movie.

Patty Jenkins, who eventually delivered the heroine in a box office hit, spent more than ten years trying to do it. In 2005, she discussed wanting to helm a Wonder Woman movie and was later sent a script, but she was pregnant and held off. In the following years, studios weren't enthusiastic when she attempted to revive the idea.

In 2012, something big happened. Lionsgate kicked off a series based on the *Hunger Games* trilogy, starring Jennifer Lawrence. The result was a huge financial success, and the concept that female-led action movies couldn't draw viewers was null and void.

Patty Jenkins directs Gal Gadot in the hit film *Wonder Woman*. It took Jenkins more than ten years to get to make the film.

Add in the need for DC to compete with Marvel's movie dominance, and there was renewed energy for the *Wonder Woman* project. Jenkins was able to step into the director's role, and actress Gal Gadot earned the lead role. The result was the highest-grossing superhero origin film to date. Perseverance truly does pay off.

Confidence, creativity, and teamwork are some of the skills a director needs, but these apply to many careers.

CHAPTER FIVE

Applying to the Real World

Now that you've seen what it takes to be a director, it might sound a bit intimidating. However, don't let that stop you from pursuing the dream! Even if you change your mind, there are a ton of benefits from giving it a try. View it as a challenge and not an impossibility, and you will reap rewards you never expected.

Ignore the Naysayers

You might hear a lot of negative talk, such as: "You're a dreamer"; "Do you know how hard it is to become a film director?"; "Are you crazy? It takes a lot of money to make a film." These and other comments can chip away at the determination of anyone wanting to be a director, even an amateur one. While there might be a grain of truth to these comments, there are ways to overcome the challenges and achieve your dream. If you have the passion and the skill, you can make it happen.

Pursuing a passion and the dream to work in television or film might be challenging, but it isn't crazy. Even if you decide later to move in a different direction, all the things you've been learning and the new ways you've stretched yourself might be the thing that makes you a perfect fit for an amazing opportunity in a completely different field.

Tools for Life

Directing takes a special blend of skills and personality to achieve success. We also know that not everyone who explores his or her potential to take on this role actually becomes a director.

Some people might get the lead role in a school play, some determined students might direct dozens of shorts to experiment with camera angles and lighting, or others could take different actions to prepare for the dream role. Even if they do this, they still might end up doing something totally different. Then there are those who do become directors but change careers after a few films. In either case, does that mean all that time and energy was wasted? Absolutely not.

Keep in mind that these tools aren't just for crafting films and shows. They are tools for life. The same confidence and poise that helps someone lead cast and crew through the filmmaking process can also help when interviewing for jobs or scholarships, giving an assigned presentation in class, applying for a car or home loan, or even asking someone out on a date. Being able to multitask and manage time prepares you for handling the pressure of high school or college studies, completing creative projects and spending time with friends between part-time jobs and chores, and juggling activities and sports.

Diligence, teamwork, multitasking, and creativity all guide people and encourage them to get more out

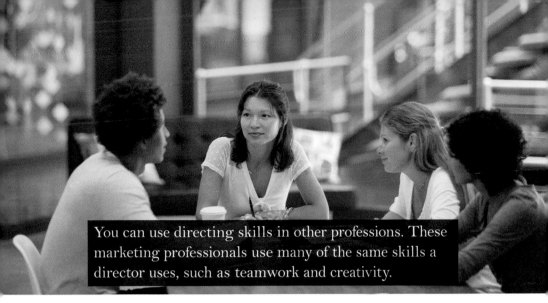

You can use directing skills in other professions. These marketing professionals use many of the same skills a director uses, such as teamwork and creativity.

of life. They inspire people to reach their goals, enjoy and perform better with recreational sports, and get the most out of a tight budget. Everything that makes a film or television production run smoothly can be applied to home, school, work, and relationships. Now, let's look at how that toolbox can lead you to a variety of career choices.

Careers

Consider for a moment each of the items in the director's toolbox (see page 86 for a refresher). You could probably come up with a dozen or more ideas to add to the list. Getting experience in film and television is a great learning ground for many jobs.

Marketing

Marketing is an excellent field for those with directing skills. Instead of being a film's champion, marketers are the champions for businesses or organizations. They promote the best qualities of a product or service and show how it can help people. Opportunities abound in this field, as almost every business and large organization has one person or an entire team devoted to marketing.

Communication, of course, is so important because speaking to an audience or potential customer in a way that encourages them to act (such as buying or signing up for more information) is the goal of marketing. Both written and verbal communication is needed, and today's marketers might be asked to host a podcast or direct a video as well as write copy for brochures and ads.

These folks must also be creative in order to make their company stand out and stay fresh in public. Teamwork is also a must as most people work in teams, with each person focusing on different areas such as social media, websites and catalogs, videos and podcasts, market research and analysis, and graphic arts. Believe it or not, even storytelling is frequently used to make a brand more personable and help it connect with its audience.

Often, marketers and filmmakers deal with stress and deadlines. Marketers have deadlines for conferences, print materials, marketing campaigns, product releases, and more. Plus, last-minute changes from corporate managers or clients are common. Developing ways of meeting deadlines and managing stress is important in any job, and having exposure to this prior to starting a career will help make you a better worker.

An advantage of the industry for someone who also loves television and film is that there are companies that focus on marketing just for entertainment. You could be helping to promote movies and shows instead of making them. This provides the best of both worlds for some people.

Event Planning

A career in event planning isn't just about birthday parties and weddings. It's also about pulling together large corporate, charity, political, and entertainment events from fundraisers and trade shows to awards ceremonies and festivals.

From decor and food to locations and entertainment, this is a busy job that requires a lot of skill and personality. Yet creativity is also needed. In fact, that is why most people hire event planners. They need someone who can put a unique theme or twist and a professional polish on an event that might otherwise be bland, boring, or poorly planned.

One must also be organized and have excellent time management skills. An event planner must juggle emails, phone calls, negotiations with service providers, and budgets; work with clients on themes and schedules; and more. Some work for a business or organization, and others are freelance and create events for a variety of customers. Once again, solid communication makes it all come together.

If this appeals to you, you are in luck: opportunities for event planners are expected to grow 11 percent over the next decade!

Human Resources

When you think about human resource managers, you probably did not see them as being anything like a director. Though most HR jobs might lack a creative outlet or storytelling flair, the position shares many other traits with filmmakers.

In human resources, you need top-notch organization and attention to detail. HR people handle a lot of official and sensitive documents related to each employee, company benefits, complaints, and more. They must understand labor laws and ensure the company is following them. Communication plays a big part, and those in HR must be able to translate information for corporate officers, management, and employees alike.

When you understand that human resource departments also handle arguments between employees or between an employee and management, you can see that it's a position that needs careful handling and decision-making skills. Plus, hiring and firing activities are stressful and require a combination of seeing a situation from different perspectives and using your instinct to find the best solution.

This career might lack the creativity that some are seeking, but it is perfect for those who excel in the organization and communication parts of filmmaking. Plus, there's no shortage of jobs in the field.

Project Management

This is another career many might not believe uses any directorial skills, but they would be wrong. After all, what is a film or TV show production if not a large team project?

Project managers put order to something that has many parts and specialties in order to meet a deadline with any given project. These professionals could be managing the creation of a website, a new product (or several products at one time), or something else, but it's really about managing the team that produces the product.

For example, a company that makes and sells its own products might have a research and development manager, product engineer, technical writer, quality assurance tester, graphic artist, package designer, and marketers involved in the creation of any given product. Each person would have a deadline for their part of the process, and any one person could throw the schedule off and cause the team to miss opportunities.

The project manager keeps all these parts of development moving on schedule and communicates the product status and key information to people. They often help shape the flow of development to be efficient and to ensure a quality product. They might even make sure the project stays on budget as well as on deadline. Understanding and learning new technology is a plus, as there are different software tools for product management.

People who excel at this job are go-getters with good personalities, because they need to stay on top of things and be someone others want to work with.

Publishing and Journalism

It might be hard to see how a world built on the written word is comparable to the visual medium of filmmaking, but it is. Whether publishing newspapers, magazines, web articles, or books, there's a lot to connect them to film and TV directing.

First, they require storytelling magic. Movies and television shows tell a story. So do magazines, books, and newspapers. The creative impulse to share a part of human nature through storytelling comes through whether it's a fictional movie or a feature article about a local beekeeper. Without a story element, they'd both be boring.

Deadline pressure is constant in publishing and journalism, as well as a need to communicate clearly and to work in teams. Yes, writers usually work alone, but they sometimes do work in teams, called cooperative writing. Beyond the writer, there are news managers/content editors, copy editors, publishers, photographers, and artists that all have a part and must work together.

A bonus of this field is that those with a passion for and understanding of film and television could specialize in reviews, entertainment news, or even celebrity biographies.

Television

One way to stay close to the fast-paced action and medium of television is to still work in the industry—just not as a director. Many local news stations and broadcast channels have someone in charge of the content that appears on screen. This is called the program director or news director. They need a lot of the same tools as a director. Making quick decisions about what stories or content to cover and then making editing decisions with a deadline looming is a daily occurrence.

Good written and verbal communication is a must for both the stories they help polish and deliver to the viewers and to staff via memos, meetings, and the constant communication required to keep things rolling at a fast pace. Camera experience and handling unusual hours is also helpful.

Teacher

If directors are the masters of channeling chaos into funnels for the entertainment industry, then teachers are the masters of the same thing in the classroom. Often overlooked because we are familiar with teaching but rarely see all that it requires, teachers or professors require a ton of confidence and creativity. Standing before a room full of important eyes, energetically delivering a lesson that you developed to further students' growth and understanding of the world, is a tall order. Now, throw in the pressure of grading and preparing lessons after school, settling student quarrels, directing project groups, and communicating with parents and school administrators. After all that, filmmaking might look easy!

Passion is another connection between the two fields. Directors are passionate about telling stories that impact viewers. Teachers are passionate about helping young people grow and be successful.

If you love filmmaking but don't love the stress and requirements for television and film work, teaching offers a chance to do what you love in a different setting. Being a theater teacher keeps your toes in directing while encouraging others to explore acting, stagecraft, and other areas. A film studies teacher shares the storytelling process and examines the techniques that filmmakers use to create a memorable work—without the fuss of Hollywood.

Manufacturing Production Manager

If you've enjoyed the more technical parts of film and television, such as operating the camera and lights, learning editing and effects software, and creating sets and props, then a job as manufacturing production manager might be a role to consider. A manufacturing manager is the leader of the team that makes products. They organize production schedules, making sure that each department has time to do their part, whether it's cutting out wood pieces or soldering electrical boards or assembling all the parts into the finished product. This has to be done as efficiently as possible or the company might lose money instead of make it. When equipment breaks down or a part they need isn't available, the manager has to think of creative solutions to get the job done.

Understanding what each department adds to the process is important, and they have often worked in those jobs before becoming a manager. They must also communicate well and inspire their manufacturing team to do good work and do it quickly in order to stay competitive.

So to sum it up, a production manager must lead while working within a team, problem-solve and manage time well, have good communication and motivational skills, and have an aptitude for technical work. It doesn't sound too different from the juggling a director must do!

These are just a handful of careers that would be awesome alternatives to a directing career while using many of the same strengths. Plus, most wouldn't require being away from home for weeks or months at a time. They can all be rewarding and more financially secure than working in the film or television industry.

Go Grab a Camera and Start Your Future!

If you love telling stories through moving pictures and have the drive and creativity to figure out how to do things, then grab a camera and go do it! Using friends and family as cast and crew will help you figure out how to work with different personalities. Not ready to handle a cast and crew? Tell your stories through stop motion—plenty of modern films like *The Boxtrolls* and *Kubo and the Two Strings* have used stop motion. You may have to shoot with your cell phone, but you will still learn to use the various shots and develop an eye for what looks good. It will also teach you dedication and patience.

Don't worry too much about what others think of the results. Let yourself experience the excitement and reward of creating a film. Regardless of what you pursue after high school, you will reap many rewards from taking a chance and pushing yourself to learn new things.

THE DIRECTOR'S TOOLBOX

Impressive. That's one way to describe the director's toolbox of skills and traits. To learn them and put them to use takes time and dedication.

So let's look at the skills and traits a future director should develop:

- Confidence

- Diligence

- Time management

- Communication with different types of people

- Decision making

- Multitasking

- Creativity

- Nonlinear thinking

- Teamwork

- Storytelling

It doesn't matter if you choose to continue on the road to Hollywood or indie film legend or instead turn down a completely different path. Developing the skills needed to be a film or television director proves beneficial no matter where life leads you. The fact is that the group of skills and strengths that directors master is needed in many other fulfilling careers.

If you want to be the one to sit in this chair, start building your director's toolbox now.

Building confidence and creativity through performing in plays or writing and directing a short film can serve anyone well, whether they work in sales, education, writing, or film. Pushing yourself to learn how to use a camera and do basic video editing proves that you can learn other technical subjects that you need to go after a dream. Being both a good team leader and team member will make you invaluable to employers, clients, and creative partners.

Any strength an amateur director has can be repurposed in other areas, so be creative and learn how to use these tools to help you create a life that you love!

GLOSSARY

blocking The movement by actors during a scene; usually the director and director of photography choose this and fine-tune it with the actors.

call sheet A document with daily shooting logistics, distributed to all cast and crew.

close-up A tight shot of the subject, showing the head and shoulders or an even smaller space.

dailies The unedited footage from a day's shooting.

director The creative leader of a television or film production; they do a number of tasks including casting, setting style, leading rehearsals and shoots, and supervising. postproduction.

establishing shot A very wide shot used to start a new scene and establish a location.

extreme close-up A shot that is so tight as to focus on one small part of the subject, such as the eyes.

50/50 A shot showing two subjects facing each other in the scene.

first assistant director This person works with the director on storyboarding, supervises cast and crew, handles the practical parts of a shoot, and keeps the filming on schedule.

indie A term for an independent film; a film made outside of the typical film studio system.

location A place from the real world that is rented for filming.

long shot Also called a wide shot; a shot that is far enough away to show the whole subject and some of the setting.

medium shot One of the most common shots; it shows the subject from head to waist.

over-the-shoulders A shot where the camera looks over the shoulder of one actor and focuses on another actor.

pan A shot where the camera pivots horizontally to follow a subject or show a distance.

point of view A shot that shows what the character is looking at.

rough cut The film or show after its initial edit. This will be rough because there will still be more editing and adding of sound and effects.

second assistant director This person moves cast through makeup and wardrobe, is in charge of creating the call sheet, and assists the assistant director.

short Another term for short film; these are less than forty minutes long and are often made by student directors.

showrunner An executive producer; the person with the creative authority on a television show.

storyboarding The act of creating a series of illustrations that helps the crew visualize how a scene will be shot.

third assistant director Coordinates and prepares the extras on a set and keeps the public off the set.

tilt A shot that is like a pan shot but vertical; shows something from top to bottom by tilting the camera from down to up or vice versa.

tracking A shot where the camera moves along with the subject. This is usually achieved with a camera dolly.

turnaround When both the camera and the lights on a set must be moved to continue filming; it's ideal to have as few turnarounds as possible.

FOR MORE INFORMATION

Books

Blofield, Robert. *How to Make a Movie in 10 Easy Lessons: Learn How to Write, Direct, and Edit Your Own Film without a Hollywood Budget.* Lake Forest, CA: Walter Foster Jr., 2015.

Herman, Sarah. *Brick Flicks: A Comprehensive Guide to Making Your Own Stop-Motion LEGO Movies.* New York: Skyhorse Publishing, 2014.

Lanier, Troy, and Clay Nichols. *Filmmaking for Teens: Pulling Off Your Shorts.* Studio City, CA: Michael Wiese Productions, 2010.

Shulman, Mark, and Hazlitt Krog. *Attack of the Killer Video Book, Take 2: Tips & Tricks for Young Directors.* Buffalo, NY: Annick Press Ltd., 2012.

Willoughby, Nick. *Digital Filmmaking for Kids for Dummies.* Hoboken, NJ: John Wiley & Sons, Inc., 2015.

Websites

Anatomy of a Scene
https://www.nytimes.com/video/anatomy-of-a-scene
See inside the mind of a director through two-to-three-minute videos of directors walking viewers through a scene from one of their recent films.

No Film School
https://www.nofilmschool.com
On this website, a community of filmmakers and creative people share and learn from each other via articles on camera technology, world building, stop motion, money-saving tips, and more.

Screenplays for You
https://www.sfy.ru
This website is a resource for finding screenplays for educational use. It posts screenplays from new and classic films in alphabetical order.

Videos

8 ESSENTIAL Skills You Need for a Career in Filmmaking
https://www.youtube.com/watch?v=1grxjdy831g
This video explores eight traits it's good to develop if you want to go into filmmaking.

Shots vs. Set Ups
https://www.youtube.com/watch?v=Q3yppt_h6bI&list=PLw_JAmvzR_MDWOxs_mMp21ShaW_RFzzbv&index=6
Learn here the difference between shots and set ups and how each works to create a smooth movie scene.

Online Articles

Forshee, Jessica. "How to Become a Film Director." Backstage.com. October 30, 2017. https:// www.backstage.com/backstage-guides/how-become-film-director.

Koo, Ryan. "10 Reasons Not to Go to Film School." No Film School. August 5, 2015. https://www. nofilmschool.com/2014/11/10-reasons-not-to-go-film-school-practical-guide-impractical-decision-jason-b-kohl.

Vineyard, Jennifer. "Nicole Holofcener on the Difference Between Directing Movies and TV." *Vulture*. October 9, 2013. http://www.vulture. com/2013/10/nicole-holofcener-on-directing-tv-vs-movies.html.

Weiss, Joanna. "What Do Television Directors Do?" Slate. April 15, 2010. http://www.slate.com/articles/arts/television/2010/04/what_do_tv_directors_do.html.

INDEX

ABOUT THE AUTHOR

PJ Graham is a freelance education writer and blogger. She worked for more than twenty years as a writer and editor for an education company and several newspapers, writing educational activity books and user guides as well as feature articles and entertainment reviews. A longtime movie buff, Graham became intrigued by the filmmaking process through two people: a former coworker who started a film production company and her stepdaughter, who is interested in pursuing a career in film. Graham lives in southeast Kansas with her family and several pets. She enjoys hiking, photography, gardening, hand drumming, and travel.